ABRAHAM ZOBELL'S HOME MOVIE: FINAL REEL...

Len Jenkin

BROADWAY PLAY PUBLISHING INC
New York
www.broadwayplaypublishing.com
info@broadwayplaypublishing.com

ABRAHAM ZOBELL'S HOME MOVIE: FINAL
REEL…
© Copyright 2017 by Len Jenkin

Cover art: *Awake O Sleepers* by Len Jenkin

First printing: May 2017
I S B N: 978-0-88145-674-5

Book design: Marie Donovan
Publishing: Adobe InDesign
Typeface: Palatino

The world premiere of ABRAHAM ZOBELL'S HOME MOVIE: FINAL REEL... opened on 18 January 2014, produced by Undermain Theatre in Dallas. The cast and creative contributors were:

STELLA .... Katherine Bourne
SISTER FLEETA .... Rhonda Boutté
UNCLE MONDAY .... Jonathan Brooks
ABRAHAM ZOBELL .... Fred Curchack
LENNY .... Teddy Davey
CLARENCE "NITEOWL" PHILLIPS,
VINCENT PRICE .... Bruce DuBose
NAT FELDMAN, RABBI MOSHOWITZ .... R Bruce Elliott
ANNA, MRS PATEL, MRS WINK .... Laura Jorgensen
CRYSTAL .... Mikaela Krantz
RODNEY PINKHAM JR. .... Rob Menzel
LULU .... Miranda Parham
CAPTAIN LARGO .... Paul Semrad
ARTHUR WINK .... Marcus Stimac
YUKI .... Stefanie Tovar

Director .... Katherine Owens
Visual consultant .... John Arnone
Sound designer .... Bruce DuBose
Video designer .... Austin Switser
Costume designer .... Giva Taylor
Properties designer .... Robert Winn
Lighting designer .... Steve Woods

CHARACTERS

CRYSTAL
YUKI
UNCLE MONDAY
SISTER FLEETA
ABRAHAM ZOBELL
ANNA ZOBELL
LARRY DUBROW
LENNY
NAT FELDMAN
LULU
STELLA
MRS PATEL
ARTHUR WINK
RABBI MOSHOWITZ
MRS WINK
CHEERLEADERS

All songs in ABRAHAM ZOBELL'S HOME MOVIE: FINAL REEL... should be sung at whatever length suits an individual production. With public domain songs, this is no problem. With those songs not in the public domain, permission for fuller use needs to be obtained by the producer. The songs are, in order of appearance:

Let Me Fly— traditional, public domain
Rama Lama Ding Dong— The Edsels
Paladin, Paladin, Where Do You Roam— theme song from the T V show, *Have Gun, Will Travel*
Smoke From Your Cigarette— Lillian Leach and the Mellows
Duke of Earl— Gene Chandler
Ship of Love— Nutmegs
Popeye the Sailorman— traditional, public domain
This World Is Not My Home— traditional, public domain
Earth Angel— The Penguins
I Am a Pilgrim— traditional, public domain
Hobo John (aka *Lost John*)— traditional, public domain
In the Still of the Night— Five Satins
Hand Me Down My Walking Cane— traditional, public domain
The Wind— Diablos

The movie is *Tomb of Ligeia* (American International Pictures, 1964)

A lifetime adrift in a boat, or in old age leading a tired horse into the years— every day is a journey, and the journey itself is home.
Basho, *Narrow Road to the Deep North*

Evening cherry blossoms
I slip the inkstone back into my kimono
One last time
Kaisho

1.

*(Sister Fleeta's Dollhouse, somewhere in America. This is a
Go-Go bar with a small stage and a dancefloor. Closing time.
Two dancers, CRYSTAL and YUKI, clear the tables. They've
changed into street clothes: CRYSTAL's a peroxide blonde,
YUKI dark-haired. Neither of them is over 25. They ain't had
it easy, and it shows.)*

*(At one table, UNCLE MONDAY is asleep, head on his arms.
He's in a ragged suit and tie, unshaven, glasses. He's pissed
himself, or is that beer? He snores.)*

*(SISTER FLEETA, an old woman in a housedress and dark
glasses, is at a keyboard near the small stage. She's blind.
She plays and sings to herself. She's smoking, ashtray on the
keyboard, and occasionally frees up one hand from playing to
feel for the cigarette, takes a drag.)*

SISTER FLEETA: *(Sings)*
Oh let me fly, oh let me fly
Let me fly to Mount Zion, Lord, Lord

Way down yonder in the middle of the field,
Angel working at the chariot wheel,
Not so particular 'bout working at the wheel,
Just want to see how the chariot feel

Oh let me fly, oh let me fly
Let me fly to Mount Zion, Lord, Lord
(Continuing under)

CRYSTAL: *(To audience)* You're at Sister Fleeta's
Dollhouse, off a two-lane blacktop, edge of town,

somewhere in America. The ocean's a few miles down the road. *(Looks at watch)* 4:10 in the A M.

(YUKI clears the last glasses from a table.)

YUKI: Another night of bliss.

CRYSTAL: Indeed.

YUKI: Assholes.

CRYSTAL: On it goes, and it goes on.

YUKI: Things to do. Places to be. Zobell.

CRYSTAL: What about him?

YUKI: He'll die soon. At home, on the road, or in the sea.

CRYSTAL: That's not certain. You can't see that far.

YUKI: What will be, Crystal honey, will be. *(She heads for the door.)* I'm gone.

SISTER FLEETA: Goodnight, sweetheart. Behave yourself out there.

YUKI: I always do. Till tomorrow night…

(YUKI's out the door. CRYSTAL glances at UNCLE MONDAY.)

CRYSTAL: Sister, Uncle Monday is…

SISTER FLEETA: I hear him. Wake him up and get him outta here.

(CRYSTAL shakes UNCLE MONDAY. He suddenly leaps up, grabs CRYSTAL's arm, looks at her watch.)

UNCLE MONDAY: I'm late! *(He runs for the door, then stops suddenly.)* Crystal, you were beautiful! Beautiful!

CRYSTAL: You were dead drunk before I even came on.

UNCLE MONDAY: Beautiful just the same. In my dreams. *(He rushes over to look at her watch again.)* The traveling hands of time! Whirling around! Makes me dizzy...

(SISTER FLEETA *plays a threatening chord.*)

UNCLE MONDAY: You ladies gonna miss me when...

(And SISTER FLEETA *plays another.)*

(UNCLE MONDAY's *out the door.*)

CRYSTAL: Get you anything before I go, Sister? A drink or...?

SISTER FLEETA: Not a thing, Crystal darlin'. I got everything I need.

CRYSTAL: Yuki said that Zobell...

SISTER FLEETA: That girl don't know everything there is to know.

CRYSTAL: I'll lock up on my way out.

SISTER FLEETA: Sweetheart, working with people is like working with bees. Sometimes you get the honey, and...

CRYSTAL: ...sometimes all you get is the sting. Goodnight.

(CRYSTAL *goes to the door. She flips the light switch. Darkness. We hear the door shut behind her.)*

(SISTER FLEETA *takes a drag. The burning tip of her cigarette is the only point of light.)*

SISTER FLEETA: It begins again. In the dark. All the same to me. *(She plays, her voice rising. Sings)*
I heard me a rumbling in the sky
I thought my Lord was passing by
Was just that chariot drawing nigh
It shook the earth and it shook the sky

Oh let me fly, oh let me fly
Let me fly to Mount Zion, Lord, Lord...

2.

(A living room. Dozing in an armchair is ABRAHAM
ZOBELL, *early 70s. He's got an I V needle in his arm,
attached to a bag of fluid on a stand near him. He's in
pajamas. On the couch a woman with long white hair
has fallen asleep. This is* ANNA. *She's in her sixties,
still beautiful. The T V is on, sound low. In the corner, a
refrigerator.)*

(Stepping quietly into this scene, so as not to wake anyone,
YUKI.*)*

YUKI: The house of Zobell! That's Abraham Zobell—
husband, English teacher, father, lover.

*(*ZOBELL *stirs in his sleep.* YUKI *reads the label on his I V
bag.)*

YUKI: Basic hydration, plus clindamycin and a touch
of morphine. His wife Anna is asleep on the couch.
On T V, a young woman holds earrings up to her ears.
Nineteen ninety-five.
All this near the dead end of Halibut Street in the
town of Hidden River. The time is 4:15 A M on a
Wednesday, in the month of November.

*(*ZOBELL *stirs again, stretches, opens his eyes.)*

YUKI: Look! Zobell wakes. Listen!

ZOBELL: *(Taking in the audience)* What can I tell you?
My name is Abraham Zobell. I'm a man like other men.
I've grown old. Bad enough. Then I got sick. Fucking
heart operation. You don't know where the hell you
are, or who— your body's light, floating…
Doctor Berger told me I was dead on the table for two
and a half minutes. I returned to the land of the living.
Small miracle. There must be something left for me to
do here.
They just sent me home yesterday.

Old and sick. A sweet release. Nothing to desire but
food and sleep. You don't even have to let it all go. It
lets go of you.
And yet…I thought, this afternoon, that I wanted to see
the ocean, one more time. Tidepools. In one is a white
anemone, and a crab, big as my thumb, the two of
them stranded in that shallow puddle in the sand.
I asked Anna to drive me to the beach.

(ANNA *sits up on the couch.*)

ANNA: That's crazy, Abe.

ZOBELL: Come on, Anna. I'll be careful. We can…

ANNA: Abe, you're not supposed to exert yourself.
In the least. You heard Doctor Berger. You'd end up
getting out of the car and chasing sandpipers. I refuse
to watch you drop dead on the beach.

ZOBELL: Anna, it's only ten miles away…

ANNA: Take your medicine, walk a little around the
house, till everything starts to heal.

ZOBELL: I know, I know…

ANNA: Abe, I'm used to you. I don't want to go
stepping out to find another man.

(*A silence between* ANNA *and* ZOBELL.)

ANNA: Abe…you feel O K?
Any pain?

ZOBELL: No.

ANNA: Then what's wrong?

ZOBELL: Are you kidding? I had a heart attack,
remember.

ANNA: I know you, Abe. There's something else. You
won't tell me, I'm not gonna push it.

ZOBELL: There's nothing else.

ANNA: You are gonna get better, Abe. The doctors said so.

ZOBELL: Sure I am. *(Points to I V)* Maybe the dope is getting to me.

ANNA: I still love you, Abe. Don't leave me... *(She lies back down on the couch, sleeps.)*

(ZOBELL looks over at ANNA to make sure she's out, then fumbles with his I V line.)

YUKI: Uh oh. Mister Zobell disconnects his I V line from his arm where the needle is taped in. Thus unencumbered, he gets up, pulls on his camelhair topcoat over his pajamas.

(ZOBELL does so.)

(Then he grabs the yellow pages, flips through...)

ZOBELL: Anna hid the damn car keys...taxi...taxi...ah! "Dubrow's Taxi Service. We take you anywhere." *(He glances at his watch.)* 4:30 A M. What the hell.

(ZOBELL dials. Ring. In another space, LARRY DUBROW in his underwear. He staggers to his phone, picks up...)

DUBROW: Who the fuck is this?

ZOBELL: I need a taxi.

DUBROW: You know what time it is?

ZOBELL: I got an emergency here. I need to get to the beach. See the ocean.

DUBROW: That's the emergency?

ZOBELL: Correct.

DUBROW: It's almost winter.

ZOBELL: Correct again.

DUBROW: Where's the pick-up?

ZOBELL: 33 Halibut Lane. Hidden River.

DUBROW: By any chance, is this Mister Zobell? Abraham Zobell?

ZOBELL: Correct for the third time. Give the man a cigar.

DUBROW: I recognize the voice.

ZOBELL: If I had a cigar. Damn doctors don't let me…

DUBROW: Distinctive. I was in your English class. 11th grade.

ZOBELL: Dubrow. Larry Dubrow! You never read *any* of *King Lear*, did you?

DUBROW: Listen, Mister Zobell. I'm not gonna take you to the ocean, or anywhere else. I'm the only taxi in town, and your wife called me yesterday. You're not supposed to go out without doctor's permission.

ZOBELL: I have doctor's permission.

DUBROW: Bullshit, Mister Zobell. Not with a massive heart attack. My brother Harry had one of those, and a week after the operation he keels over in his driveway. No one even knew he was lying there till his wife drove over him when she came home from the beauty parlor.

ZOBELL: Yeah, well, I'm sorry to hear that, Larry.

DUBROW: Don't be. Harry was a mean son-of-a-bitch, especially to Evelyn.

ZOBELL: Who's Evelyn?

DUBROW: His wife. She moved to Fort Myers, down in Florida.

ZOBELL: Larry.

DUBROW: I'm not gonna do it, Mister Zobell.

ZOBELL: Thanks anyway, Larry.

DUBROW: Take care, Mister Z. We used to wonder how you could love those books so much.

ZOBELL: What?

DUBROW: You were my favorite teacher. *(He disappears.)*

(ZOBELL hangs up, opens the fridge, begins to put food into a bag. YUKI looks on.)

YUKI: Provisions.

ZOBELL: For the road. Oscar Meyer bologna, half a loaf of whole wheat, Gulden's mustard…

YUKI: Heading out for the territory…

ZOBELL: Side of bacon, sack of cornmeal, jug of whiskey.

YUKI: Wool hat, boots.

(ZOBELL puts those on. He picks up a small video camera.)

ZOBELL: Video. So they can see, those to come, where I went, and how I traveled.

(ZOBELL puts the camera in his pocket. He looks around the room, spots a vase of cut flowers. He takes a few, puts one alongside Anna's sleeping face, so she'll see it when she wakes. He puts the others carefully in his inside coat pocket.)

(He tiptoes to the door.)

YUKI: Anna doesn't know yet that her husband disappears. That will happen soon enough. At the moment, she's dreaming, and Baba Yaga, Death's witch, crashes into her dream. Her eyes are bright blue pinwheels. She's screaming into the wind, mouth open, teeth all rotted away. Her saliva is flecked with gold. Anna cries out from her dream…

ANNA: Abe! Abe!

(ZOBELL doesn't move. ANNA sleeps on.)

ZOBELL: *(Softly)* Anna, I love you. *(He's gone.)*

3.

(Upstage a large screen. On it appears the black and white video that ZOBELL *is shooting as he walks, the record of his journey. It parallels the time of day and the roadside landscape he tells us about. It does not show any of the people he meets on the road. They appear live.)*

(The video travels at a walker's pace, stops for a scene to play out, zooms in to let us have a close look at something, responding to ZOBELL's *walk and the onstage action.)*

(The basic video content is what you'd see off any two lane blacktop: patchy woods, billboards, suburban houses, strip malls, and later on, the seaside.)

*(*ZOBELL *steps out into the night.)*

ZOBELL: Fucking cold. I ripped out the I V needle pulling my topcoat on. Bleeding down my arm. Maybe I'm leaving a trail of blood.
Follow me, if you can…

*(*ZOBELL *raises the video camera to his eye. Video begins rolling on the screen behind him.)*

ZOBELL: The streets in this neighborhood are named after fish. Halibut Lane, Pike Street, Cod Road, Bluefish Boulevard along the railroad tracks, Eel Ave, Neptune Parkway down to the sea.
(Sings)
By the sea, by the sea, by the beautiful sea, you and me, you and me, oh how happy we'll be…
To Beaches, hang a left. Signs and wonders. I am under a streetlight, crescent moon through the thin clouds. First drops of rain in the dark…
Zobell. My name is written in salt, gonna wash away in the rain. Dump who I am like an old suit of clothes. Give it to the ragman, baby, I don't need it anymore. I'm a very mutable guy.

"Ain't you the sweetie-pie? All the girls must be in love, L U V"

So true, baby, but right now I need a few things on the local level— pair of Keds, a ham on rye, some quarters to feed the meter. I'll be on the planet for awhile, out here in this half-deleted landscape, my last autumn, strolling down to the sea.

One foot up, toenail dragging, haul me away in the hoodoo wagon...

My mother died when I was a baby. My father, Murray Zobell, spent his days bent over pockets with holes. A tailor. He barely spoke to me. One night when I was ten years old, my father sat in the kitchen sucking on a quart of slivovitz he'd been given for relining a coat. He looked over at me like he'd never seen me before. Then he said, "Your mother was sick for weeks. I had no money for the doctor. A bad winter. No heat, and the radiators clanked all night. We couldn't sleep. She lay in bed next to me. Her lips were blue. She began to breathe heavy, like there was a stone on her chest. Take care of Abie, she said, and turned her face to the wall. She was only a child. Eighteen years old.

What kind of world is this that God made, little Abie? Tell me.

(Silence)

(A man appears, long white beard, dark glasses, holding a mop: LENNY.)

LENNY: Hey kid! What you doin' out here?

ZOBELL: Hey, its Lenny! Hey, Lenny! It's been years! How you been?

LENNY: Its late, kid. Nitetime. And you're out here telling stories.

ZOBELL: Lenny! Are you...

LENNY: Everything's closed, kid. You shouldn't be onna street by yourself.

ZOBELL: I can't drive anymore, Lenny.

LENNY: Too many creeps.

ZOBELL: The doctors won't let me. Anna hid the keys. Hey, Lenny, you remember that '57 Buick Riviera I had. The clutch blew. I sold it to the junkyard.

LENNY: Too bad, kid. That was a nice set of wheels.

ZOBELL: I'm going to see the ocean. You wanna go down there with me?

LENNY: I'm busy, kid. I gotta oil the machinery of heaven.

ZOBELL: You what?

LENNY: If I don't do the job, the spheres rub against each other, and you get that shivery-wivery sound, makes your soul ache down to your toes. Also, I gotta take the trash off the pier. *(He turns to go.)*

ZOBELL: Hey, Lenny, wait up…

(LENNY's gone.)

ZOBELL: There's a pier at the beach. Feldman's Amusements. I worked there my last three summers of high school. In the Haunted Castle.
Enter if you dare!
I was the cook at the Transylvania Grill. I didn't even have to apply for the job,…

(NAT FELDMAN appears, middle aged, bad suit and tie.)

NAT FELDMAN: I seen you hanging around the pier looking at the girls with your thumb up your ass. I'm Nat Feldman, and I need a schmuck like you. You put frozen burgers on the grill, slap 'em on a bun and serve the clientele. Don't burn yourself. I don't need the hassle with the hospital. Take the job, kid, or you'll

spend the summer pulling your doodle. Besides, the
pay is primo excellento for talent like yourself. I, Nat
Feldman, wouldn't fuck with you. I am the original
solid sender.

Talk to me. We open the Haunted Castle in a week.

ZOBELL: Well, Mister Feldman, I...

NAT FELDMAN: Boo!

ZOBELL: The grill was right next to the fryolator and the
freezer. I made coffee in a Mr Coffee. Slow nights I'd
take a couple nembutal and ride the Octopus.

NAT FELDMAN: No dope in the castle!

ZOBELL: The pier had kiddie rides, a carousel, a
contortionist guy from Bulgaria who rammed railroad
spikes up his nose. And Mademoiselle Electra. She
went to my high school. Lulu. She was a dancer, took
modern dance classes somewhere. She was beautiful,
sitting in that electric chair in a red bikini.

(LULU *appears, as described.*)

LULU: Hey, Abie! Abie the grillman!

(LULU *flips a switch. ZAP! A crackling sound, blue sparks,
as electricity stands her hair on end. She laughs and waves.*)

ZOBELL: Same old spider
Same old web
Neural circuits light up like
Xmas in the blood
Frozen custard stand
Flies buzz in the heat
Tiny freckles across her nose
She looks me over and she laughs
And then a great quiet descends From Heaven.
Even in this supernatural silence,
Somebody gotta start the conversation—

Gimme two creamsicle swirls
And a coffee...
And after we close
Her tongue in my mouth
End of the pier
Out over the water

(LULU's *gone.* LENNY *reappears, mopping.*)

ZOBELL: Nat Feldman came around one night and told me about Lenny...

(*And* NAT FELDMAN *does.*)

NAT FELDMAN: Burned his brains out on sockadelic drugs, my personal charity case. Lenny mops out, picks up the trash. I gave him a room out there on the pier. Sometimes he prowls around at night— don't let him spook you.

(NAT FELDMAN's *gone.* LENNY *looks up, sees* ZOBELL.)

LENNY: Lemme ask you a question, kid. Can a man help who he is? Can he make himself someone God didn't make him?

ZOBELL: I fry burgers, Lenny. Ask a priest. Or a rabbi.

LENNY: You're smart as them, kid. Smart as anyone. You could even be a teacher. (*He keeps mopping.*)

ZOBELL: Its closed now, the pier. I drove by there last summer, mid July. Had a For Sale sign on the place, Haunted Castle and all. (*He walks a few steps, video rolling. He clutches his chest. He's shaking, swaying back and forth.*)

(CRYSTAL *appears. She's wearing a nurse's cap.*)

CRYSTAL: Sorry to see you back with us so soon, Mister Zobell.

ZOBELL: Where am I? Who are...

CRYSTAL: Walking to the ocean? That is beyond stupid, Mister Zobell. And dangerous. If you don't care about yourself, what about Anna?

ZOBELL: Get me my medicine, please.

CRYSTAL: You should have just remembered the waves...or had a dream...

LENNY: What's wrong with the kid, nurse? What's he doing out here on the road? He should be home in bed...

(ZOBELL *recovers, a few deep breaths, steadies himself.*)

(CRYSTAL *and* LENNY *are gone.*)

(ZOBELL *walks a few hesitant steps, pauses.*)

ZOBELL: No cars, nothing moves in the translucent dark. There's a music store in that stripmall across the road, speaker must have been left on all night...

(*Night stripmall on screen.* ZOBELL *listens, music dim and far away: Neil Young's* Heart of Gold.)

(ZOBELL *continues under*)

ZOBELL: Paladin, paladin, where do you roam?
I'll die on this road, under a streetlight, head in a puddle.
Hey, man, at least the poor bastard gave it a shot—
A fool in the forest, lost,
The bells on his cap tinkle.
Night falls.
First light in the east
Sun rises out of the sea.
Where I'm going.
There's a 7-11 up ahead. I got money. They got coffee.

4.

(*A convenience store appears onscreen.* YUKI *appears behind a register.*)

ZOBELL: Small coffee, regular…and a carton of Camel straights.

(YUKI *hands over the items.*)

YUKI: Uh— Mister, you look like shit. I can call the Highway Patrol. They'll take you to a…

ZOBELL: I'm fine. Mind your own business, please.

YUKI: I was only trying to…

(ZOBELL *rips open the carton, opens a pack, puts one in his mouth.*)

ZOBELL: Haven't had a smoke in thirty years. Lemme fire one up here. (*He lights up, smokes, coughs.*) Once upon a time, I was an English teacher.

YUKI: Before I got behind this register, I was the Queen of Sheba.

ZOBELL: "Pillicock up on Poolacock Hill." Not quite.

(CRYSTAL *appears.*)

CRYSTAL: Abraham Zobell is on his second Camel when he remembers the quotation from Lear correctly…

ZOBELL: "Pillicock sat on Pillicock-hill: Halloo, halloo, loo, loo!"

(YUKI *is gone.* ZOBELL *walks on, shoots with camera as he smokes. Video rolls.*)

CRYSTAL: Late autumn, black fields
Corn rots on the stalk,
Food for crows
Sit silent on a branch

Under a dead sky
Far off, on the horizon
A bonfire burns...

ZOBELL: *(Sings)*
I got a girl named Rama Lama,
Rama Lama Ding Dong...

Hey little darlin'
You with the ponytail.
Call me Slick.
I'm yours.
Love me quick
Cause before you know it
I'm gone.

Up the avenue there's that
Train station
Get my shoes shined when I'm going
Somewhere.
Here's a ten spot, kid.
I need to see my reflection
In those Florsheims, remind myself
What a beautiful man I am.

(UNCLE MONDAY *appears, wearing a sandwich board
sign. It reads:* SISTER FLEETA'S DOLLHOUSE
GIRLS! GIRLS! GIRLS!*)*

UNCLE MONDAY: The one! The only! The one and only
Sister Fleeta's Dollhouse! Gorgeous girls! Sister Fleeta
at the piano for your listening pleasure!
My dear sir! Pause a moment on your foolish journey,
if you will. A gentleman of your fast fading distinction,
wandering the high road— I, Uncle Monday, am
delighted to make your acquaintance.

ZOBELL: Uncle who?

UNCLE MONDAY: Hearing problem, is it? MONDAY.

ZOBELL: What kind of a name is...

UNCLE MONDAY: Never mind that.

ZOBELL: What are you selling?

UNCLE MONDAY: The Dollhouse sells itself. Even an old sick English teacher is lured by the eternal triumvirate of desire. Cold beer, loud music, young women.

ZOBELL: 'Scuse me. I need to keep walking.

UNCLE MONDAY: Not yet.

ZOBELL: Get out of my way.

UNCLE MONDAY: You Abe Zobell? Doctor Berger sent me.

ZOBELL: Wha…

UNCLE MONDAY: A check up. Post op. (*He pulls a filthy labcoat out of his pocket, puts it on. He's got a notebook and the stub of a pencil. He licks the tip.*) I am a certified cognitive neurologist, accredited and licensed by the powers that be.
What country are you in?

ZOBELL: United States of America.

UNCLE MONDAY: Hmmm. And what month is it?

ZOBELL: November.

UNCLE MONDAY: Hmmm. Day of the week?

ZOBELL: It's Fri…Or is it…

UNCLE MONDAY: Time's chariot, drag you right along. Hour of the day?

ZOBELL: Look, I don't have to answer this crap. I…

UNCLE MONDAY: Where are you going, exactly?

ZOBELL: The ocean.

UNCLE MONDAY: Aren't we all, dancing back down to the sea? Woof! The Black Dog nips at our heels. Woof! Woof!

Same old ocean, Mister Zobell. It hasn't changed since
Noah rode it. You have Uncle Monday's blessing, not
that its worth a damn. I hope you make it, though none
of us do, you know. Everyone's got a losing hand, even
if it looks like a royal fucking flush. *(He strips off his
labcoat, tosses it away.)* Catch you later. I gotta find that
little sonofabitch. The bastard ruined my life.

ZOBELL: Who the hell are you talking about?

UNCLE MONDAY: Mister Weenie. *(Spits)* He stole her
from me— Violet Du Bosque, the pre-eminent beauty
of the age, and a helluva trick shot artiste with the bow
and arrow. He hauled her off the Cole Brothers lot in
his fucking Buick Roadmaster, with that cash he got
from the insurance scam. Demonic shrimp!
You see him, you let me know. I'm gonna rip his little
guts out and feed them to the seagulls. *(He's gone.)*

(Video rolling, ZOBELL walking.)

ZOBELL: That place I worked at when I was a kid,
Feldman's Amusements...one day I'm on break, lying
on the beach, and Nat Feldman himself rises up out of
the ocean in a plaid bathing suit, shaking the water off
himself like a dog.

*(NAT FELDMAN enters as described. He slings a towel over
his shoulders, lights a cigar.)*

ZOBELL: We stood there on the sand, looking out at the
pier.

NAT FELDMAN: Every summer I lose money. Do I give
a shit? No. You know why?
It's a work of art, kid, the whole fucking thing. Right
outta Nat Feldman's brain onto the pier. Kids come
here, they go in the Haunted Castle, they ride the rides.
Thirty years later they wake up in the night, carousel
music playing way back in their heads, almost too soft

to hear— and then their brains open like an oyster—
and there's the pearl.

ZOBELL: What pearl?

NAT FELDMAN: I used to live out there, all the way at
the end. Waves roll in forever, right under you.
Guess what, kid? They never stop. You gotta love it, or
it drives you nuts.
The rules of your life at Feldman's Amusements are
simple. Even an ignorant schmuck like you, Zobell,
and I say that with love, can understand them. Show
up on time, fryolater to medium, stay off the dope,
chase the girls.
Little Lulu is something else. I noticed you noticed.
Nice kid. Treat her right.

ZOBELL: Mister Feldman, I...

NAT FELDMAN: Don't dip in the till.

(LENNY *appears, long beard, sunglasses, waving a mop.*)

LENNY: Hey Nat! Hey, kid! It's me! Lenny!

NAT FELDMAN: Retard. If I didn't keep him mopping,
he'd be in Fuck You Manor, playing checkers with
some braindead nutball.

(NAT FELDMAN's *gone.* LENNY's *gone.*)

ZOBELL: (*Spooky voice*) Enter the Haunted Castle! If you
dare! Ha ha ha ha ha ha!

(ZOBELL *shoots video as he walks.* CRYSTAL *appears.*)

CRYSTAL: Out along the blacktop
Hi-Hat Tavern
Mama Wong's Vietnamese
Boarded up storefronts
Sunoco
Rusted playgrounds
Saint Vincent De Paul Thrift Store Alvarado Tires

We Fix Flats
Mike's Sub Shop
Empty stretch of scrub
Billboard for an ambulance chaser
Bus stop.
From a distance that lonesome whistle...
And from beyond Hidden River
Long low whistle of a freight train-
The whistle fading...

(ZOBELL *stumbles, the image on screen shakes, he falls.*)

(*Screen to black*)

CRYSTAL: There's pain in his arms, and along the incision, and deep inside his chest. The train whistle fades away on the night air and he lies there alongside the blacktop, not knowing if he has the strength to stand again.

(ZOBELL *struggles, and at last he rises to his knees.*)

ZOBELL: Everything dies
Even the most beautiful things
That grace this world
And make the heart of it
They die too.

(ZOBELL *totters, about to fall back to the ground.* CRYSTAL *holds him, keeping him up on his knees.*)

CRYSTAL: Get up, Mister Abraham Zobell. You don't want Anna to find you lying in the weeds by the roadside, with the beer cans and the dog shit.
You're not done. Not here, not yet.

(CRYSTAL *gently helps* ZOBELL *up. He stands shakily, brushes himself off, slowly begins to walk.* CRYSTAL's *gone.*)

5.

(STELLA *appears, sitting on the curb, her head in her hands.*
She's maybe 19. Jeans, T-shirt, some kind of beat-up jacket.
YUKI *stands alongside her.)*

YUKI: Stella! A young lady from the other side of town.
Across the tracks...

ZOBELL: 'Scuse me. Are you O K?

STELLA: I been better.

ZOBELL: Is there anything I can...?

(STELLA *looks up at* ZOBELL.)

STELLA: Just what I need. Some old wino hitting on me.

ZOBELL: O K.
I'll be on my way...

STELLA: Fuck you.

ZOBELL: ...to the ocean.

STELLA: And fuck the ocean.

ZOBELL: Goodbye.

YUKI: The old man in the camelhair topcoat over his
pajamas keeps walking slowly east along the shoulder.
After a moment...

(STELLA *gets up, catches up to* ZOBELL, *and begins to walk*
alongside him, matching his slow pace. Video rolling. They
walk on.)

YUKI: They walk side by side in silence for about an
hour, until Abe Zobell says...

ZOBELL: Look me over, kid. You'll see the joker under
the skin. Mister Bones. I'm walking to the water cure.
Down to the ocean.
I don't mind company.

STELLA: Neither do I, Grampa.

ZOBELL: My name is Abe Zobell.

STELLA: I'm Stella.
And I might as well go your way. Better than no way at all.

(On they walk, lights coming on in strip malls, stores, houses. Early evening)

ZOBELL: Stella, you hungry?

STELLA: I'm starving.

(On screen, a Chinese restaurant. Nice neon)

YUKI: Ah! Madame Wong's Jade Palace.

ZOBELL: Lets get some take out from this chop suey joint...

(YUKI whips out two food containers, hands them to ZOBELL.)

YUKI: Chairman Mao's Chicken and the Pu-Pu Platter.

(STELLA and ZOBELL sit on a bench and eat. STELLA's got the chicken and a plastic fork.)

ZOBELL: My new companion has garlic sauce all over her chin.

STELLA: This stuff is great. *(She keeps eating.)*

ZOBELL: Along the river road
Silent houses, blinds drawn.

(LULU appears on her Mademoiselle Electra platform. Now she's in a flowing white dress.)

(She's smoking.)

ZOBELL: Lulu said...

LULU: I'm a dancer
I know who I am, a dancer.
You are the boy from the pier.
I don't know how you got into my bedroom.

But now that you're here
You can never leave...

(Music. LULU *stubs out her cigarette, steps down off the platform and dances, simple modern dance. She's gawky, beautiful, wonderfully expressive. The dance is melancholy, slow. She sings snatches of the lyric...)*

*(*ZOBELL *watches, transfixed. Then he sings with her, and the music.)*

ZOBELL: *(Sings)*
Doo doo doo doo...
Smoke from your cigarette
clouds my eyes...

*(*LULU *fades away, as her music continues softly...)*

YUKI: Still standing there, surrounded by the same silent houses with their blinds drawn, Lulu's dance music rises up into the windy sky...

(The music's gone.)

YUKI: Nothing changes, does it, Mister Zobell?
(She lights a cigarette.) Down at the beach, out on the pier, lights of the carousel blink out. Feldman's Amusements, closed for the night. Closed for the season. Closed till Kingdom Come.

(It starts to rain.)

*(*YUKI's *gone.* STELLA's *done eating. Rain)*

*(*ZOBELL *turns up his collar.* STELLA *shivers in the wet and cold. Thunder)*

STELLA: Uh, Mister Zobell. It's fucking pouring. Getting soaked to the skin isn't gonna be good for you— me either.

ZOBELL: I got money. We better check in someplace...

(The Neptune Motel appears onscreen. Vacancy sign flashes.)

ZOBELL: Right on time.
(Sings)
As I wander through this world,
Nothing, nothing can stop the Duke of Earl...

6.

(Neptune Motel still on screen. CRYSTAL is sitting around the motel office. STELLA and ZOBELL approach the check-in desk. MRS PATEL appears behind it.)

MRS PATEL: Welcome to the Neptune Motel. I am your solicitous proprietess, Mrs Patel.
Cash only. Sign the book.

(ZOBELL writes in a large guestbook. MRS PATEL looks down at the names.)

MRS PATEL: Father Christmas and Tinkerbelle. I am laughing. Ha ha. *(Handing over key)* Take your little whore to room seven.

STELLA: Watch your mouth, bitch.

MRS PATEL: You don't like the truth, go somewhere else.

(Huge clap of thunder. More rain)

ZOBELL: We'll stay.

MRS PATEL: Lovely.
If you hear a damp gurgling in the night, pray to your gods. Management takes no responsibility for your fate.

ZOBELL: What are you saying?

MRS PATEL: The Neptune Motel is sinking. The ground beneath us is soft— a huge bog.
Once there was a town here. It sank slowly, over the years. A few days ago, the last chimney top disappeared. Its all down there in the bog— homes,

hotels, whorehouses, banks, bars, churches. This motel was spared, but the bog slime sucks at the foundation. I can feel it even now. The moral of that story— we live on the lip of the abyss.
Good luck.
Two Kingfisher. (*Handing the bottles over to* ZOBELL)
On the house.

(CRYSTAL *and* MRS PATEL *are gone.*)

(*The room interior appears: a single bed, a nightstand, metal folding chairs. Flypaper hangs from above, along with a bare bulb.*)

(ZOBELL *sits, exhausted.*)

STELLA: You rest, Mister Zobell. I'll crack these.

(STELLA *finds a churchkey, opens the beers, hands one to* ZOBELL.)

STELLA: Cheers, Mister Zobell.

(STELLA *and* ZOBELL *drink.*)

STELLA: And good luck. I think maybe you deserve it.

ZOBELL: Thank you, Stella.
Good luck to you too.

STELLA: Good luck? I turned nineteen five days ago. If there was a party, I wasn't invited. I've been sleeping in the woods, once in a Chevron station bathroom. Unpleasant. Now I'm in a motel room with a sick old man.

ZOBELL: You could do worse.

STELLA: I probably will.

ZOBELL: What about your parents?

STELLA: What about them?

ZOBELL: Won't they be…

STELLA: They kicked me out of the house. They found this jar of speed racer hid in my underwear drawer. My ex-boyfriend made me keep it for him. Arthur Wink. I do believe he stole it from some drugstore. Total meth-head, and nasty in bed. He has a mind like a rabid raccoon.

I heard the asshole actually got a job last week. He's a Pronto Pizza delivery guy. Can you believe it?

ZOBELL: Stella...what do you think about human beings?
You know, people. Are they always selfish, or stupid, or cruel?

STELLA: I take people as they come
Some of them are nice sometimes
When they want to fuck you
Or borrow money.
You're asking me questions and
I don't even know where I'm going
I'm broke
No dope
No cigarettes
The one idea I got is
To find someone
Who'll be kind to me
And it's raining out there.

(*Long silence between* STELLA *and* ZOBELL)

STELLA: Guy like you's gotta have a wife. What's her name?

ZOBELL: Anna.
She must be worried about me.

STELLA: Didn't you tell her you were taking this stroll to the seaside?

ZOBELL: No.

STELLA: Not good, Mister Zobell.

ZOBELL: She wouldn't have let me go.
I had a heart operation. The doctors said I had to stay
home and rest.

STELLA: Whoa. She's gonna flip.
And she's gonna be pissed.

ZOBELL: I couldn't help it. I felt like any moment
something inside me could rip open again, and I'd
never get to go.
Not in this life, anyway.

STELLA: Mister Zobell, you had this big operation, and
then you go dragging your sorry old ass along the
highway in your fucking pajamas. Where the hell do
you think you're gonna get to?

ZOBELL: I told you. I want to see the ocean again, one
more time.

STELLA: Seen one wave, seen them all.

ZOBELL: Stella, don't pretend you don't understand me.

STELLA: Oh, you mean you want to see the gynormous
eternally rolling ocean, full of tunafish and whales and
the secrets of the deep.
I hate that shit.

ZOBELL: What shit? Whales?

STELLA: People lying to me.

(A long silence between STELLA and ZOBELL again.
Thunder. Sound of rain)

ZOBELL: I'm going to put flowers on a grave.

STELLA: 'Scuse me?

ZOBELL: I got 'em right here. (He goes to his coat, takes
flowers out of the inside pocket.)

STELLA: It's a beach, not a cemetery. There's no graves down there.

ZOBELL: Sailor's grave.
There was a girl. Years ago. Lulu. Her name was Lulu.

STELLA: You're trying to tell me something, Mister Zobell, but you haven't done it yet.

ZOBELL: She drowned at the beach, off the pier. Lenny saw her first. He started screaming, waving his mop in the air. I ran over to the rail, looked down. There she was, floating quietly just below the green surface of the water, face up, eyes wide open, and her dress billowed around her on the waves.
A rescue team got ready to swim out from shore. Then, as if pulled under by unseen hands, she was gone. A searchlight moved over the water. Nothing. The ocean had taken her.
She must have jumped from the pier. Or maybe she fell. I don't know. She was eighteen years old.
Why am I telling you all this?

STELLA: I asked you.

ZOBELL: So you did.
Sailor's grave.
I want to toss flowers
On the sea, say a few words to her
While I still can.

STELLA: Well then, Mister Abraham Zobell, I hope you make it.

(Low thunder. Sound of rain)

STELLA: You're a runaway. Like me. Little old for the job.
Let's see if this T V works.

(As STELLA goes toward the T V, the door to the motel room bursts open. Standing in the doorway, soaking wet, is

ARTHUR WINK. *He's about 22, jeans, Pronto Pizza Delivery jacket.)*

WINK: So this is where you been hiding, Stella darlin'. Nice. With a little fixing up, it'd be the perfect place to cut your own throat.

STELLA: Arthur, just…

WINK: Do you realize my Pronto Pizza delivery scooter is almost out of gas, checking every motel for miles. No way to treat your loving boyfriend.

STELLA: You're not my boyfriend, Arthur.

WINK: Oh indeed I am, Stella darling. Lay down on that bed over there, take off your clothes, and lets talk it over.

(WINK notices ZOBELL.)

WINK: Who's the corpse?

STELLA: He's not dead yet. His name's Abe Zobell.

WINK: Abe Zobell, get the hell outta here. I need to take my medicine. Privately. *(He takes out injection paraphernalia.)*

STELLA: Arthur, you are one fucked up creep.

WINK: I know you love me, baby. Kindly shut up while I take this hit. Then the party starts.

(Thunder. Rain)

STELLA: Arthur, please. Leave us alone.

WINK: Us? *(To ZOBELL)* Didn't I ask you politely to leave?

(WINK goes over to ZOBELL, shoves him toward the door.)

ZOBELL: It's pouring out there.

WINK: That rain makes the daffodils grow.

(WINK *shoves* ZOBELL *again.* ZOBELL *stumbles, crashes to the ground by the door. He lies still.* WINK *turns back to* STELLA.)

WINK: Don't even open your mouth, you dumb bitch. I'm in no mood for criticism.

(*In another space,* MRS PATEL *begins to pray to Ganesha in Hindi. The chant repeats, over and over, softly.*)

(WINK *sits, loads his needle from a vial, ties off, and focuses on finding a vein.*)

(ZOBELL *stands, picks up a metal folding chair, raises it high. He smashes* WINK *over the head.* WINK *buckles, starts to fall. The chair is smeared with hair and blood.* ZOBELL *throws it in a corner, and* WINK *is still falling, slow-motion, like a cow hit in the forehead with a sledge— he tries to stand, knees give, and he hits the floor. He doesn't move.*)

(ZOBELL *feels for a pulse.*)

ZOBELL: I think he's dead.

STELLA: Good job, Mister Z. Arthur would've raped me, or killed me, or both— he was a worthless bastard, and the world is better off with him out of it.

(MRS PATEL's *chant fades. She's gone.*)

STELLA: Cover him with something. I don't want to see his face.

(ZOBELL *manages to throw a bedspread over* WINK's *body.*)

(*He sits down on the bed.* STELLA *turns on the T V, flips through some channels.*)

VINCENT PRICE ON T V: Rowena! Rowena, my bride for eternity!

STELLA: I love this movie.

(CRYSTAL *reappears.*)

CRYSTAL: So do I. Vincent Price in *Tomb of Ligeia.*

(Our two travelers try to relax, even with a corpse nearby, and another on T V.)

(STELLA's glued to the screen.)

(Thunder. Rain on the roof of the motel)

(On T V, Vincent Price is mumbling in Latin and waving a silver crucifix over a shrouded dead woman. The body stirs, rises, gropes toward him!)

VINCENT PRICE: Rowena! I've brought you back, back from the dead...

(STELLA begins to play the parts.)

LIGEIA & STELLA: Verdon, my love!

(STELLA stands, and in re-animated corpse mode, shakes out her hair.)

VINCENT PRICE: Your hair! Its not blonde! Its black!

VINCENT PRICE & STELLA: Black as night! You're not Rowena! You're Ligeia! NO! NO!

(On T V, Ligeia, in her bloody burial gown, advances toward Price! STELLA does her zombie routine.)

LIGEIA & STELLA: Yes, Verdon, it is I! And you are coming with me, beyond the grave!!!

VINCENT PRICE & STELLA: No!! No!!!

ZOBELL: Turn the damn thing off.

STELLA: This is the best part.

ZOBELL: Turn it off, please.

(STELLA turns off the T V, turns to ZOBELL.)

ZOBELL: Stella...

STELLA: I'm listening.

ZOBELL: About Lulu, that girl I told you about...the one who drowned...

STELLA: You gonna tell me you loved her?

ZOBELL: Yes, I am.

STELLA: I already knew that.

(*A long beat between* STELLA *and* ZOBELL)

ZOBELL: Lulu got pregnant that summer, right after
high school. I was going off to college in the fall. She
wanted us to stay together, to have the baby... old
story, isn't it?

STELLA: Only so many love stories under the sun,
Mister Zobell. When your turn comes around, they're
all brand new.

(ZOBELL *falls silent for another long beat. It's a hard story
for him to tell.* STELLA *waits patiently for him to begin.*)

ZOBELL: Me and Lulu.
Lulu and me.
We worked on the pier at Feldman's Amusements,
always took our breaks together. The night she died,
we had a fight. Lulu was cursing at me, and then she
was crying. Her whole body was shaking. I didn't
know if I wanted to stay, or go.
I walked away. I turned once to look back at her. She
was still standing there under that yellow streetlight,
quiet and still, like a ghost.
My shift wasn't over till midnight, so I went back to
work at the grill. This doo-wop station was on the
radio. I just leaned on the counter like a fucking idiot,
listening to all these pathetic love songs, feeling sorry
for Lulu and sorrier for myself.
That's when I heard Lenny screaming, and ran over to
the rail.

STELLA: You know what? I knew all that already,
Mister Zobell. Like I remembered it.

ZOBELL: No you didn't, Stella. It all happened before
you were born.

STELLA: I knew it anyway, even about the radio station... *(Sings)*
I sit in my room
Looking out at the rain...

ZOBELL: That which has been will be
And that which is to be
Has already been—
On the local level
Shit never stops happening
In the big picture, chances are
Nothing's happening.
Nothing at all.
(He lies back down in bed, tries to sleep.)

(STELLA kneels by the bedside.)

STELLA: For my mother and father, poor Mister Zobell, and me, Stella. We could use plenty of it. Let it fall.

ZOBELL: Let what fall?

STELLA: God's mercy.

ZOBELL: Amen.

(STELLA gets into bed alongside ZOBELL, her back to him.)

STELLA: Goodnight, Mister Abe Zobell.

CRYSTAL: Our intrepid travelers fall asleep at last. No damp gurgling can be heard. The Neptune Motel won't sink into the bog, not tonight anyway.
Meanwhile, on Feldman's Amusement Pier, out over the ocean, Lenny is at the rail. He leans out into the darkness.

(In another space, LENNY)

LENNY: My head is a fish.

CRYSTAL: Far off across the water, the tiny lights of a boat move out to sea, getting smaller and smaller. They're gone.

LENNY: Whoosh! Disappeared!
(Sings)
The ship of love
Carries you from me…
(He begins to dance, and sing another song.)
(Sings)
I'm Popeye the sailor man!
I'm Popeye the sailor man!…

7.

(CRYSTAL, YUKI, and SISTER FLEETA at her keyboard.)

(Sister Fleeta's Dollhouse appears around them.)

(At a table, LENNY and RABBI MOSHOWITZ. He is a middle aged man in a bad suit and tie, wearing a yarmulke. LENNY has his usual Z Z Top style beard, dark glasses, and has his mop with him.)

SISTER FLEETA: Is all that local clientele outta here?

YUKI: Yes ma'am. I persuaded them to go home.

SISTER FLEETA: Don't hurt nobody, Yuki. I don't know about you sometimes.
Who's left in the house?

YUKI: Lenny and Rabbi Moshowitz over there.

SISTER FLEETA: Leave 'em stay till your rat killing's done.
Crystal?

CRYSTAL: Yes, Sister?

SISTER FLEETA: How's our friend Zobell doing?

CRYSTAL: Still on the road.

SISTER FLEETA: Keep an eye on him. He's carrying a lot of weight…

YUKI: He killed someone.

SISTER FLEETA: We talking about Zobell here?

YUKI: No joke, sister. A man named Arthur Wink.

SISTER FLEETA: Wink...I remember that monkey's asshole. Good riddance.

CRYSTAL: Zobell deserves to have his burdens lifted. He's been a good man.

YUKI: Good? Has all that goodness made the tide turn? Or the bloodshed end?

CRYSTAL: He's done his best. A faithful servant.

YUKI: Faithful, bullshit. He's a man like other men. No better, not much worse.

SISTER FLEETA: Quiet, ladies. Sounds like baby birds in the nest. Peep peep peep...
We'll see what we'll see.
(Sings and plays)
This world is not my home
I'm only passing through
My treasures are laid up
Somewhere beyond the blue
The angels beckon me
From heaven's open door
And I can't feel at home
In this world anymore...
(Continuing under)

CRYSTAL: Night on earth.
Somebody's frying chicken
Cold beer
Dinner under the trees
Old dog gets up slow to chase a
Chipmunk, who disappears
Under the woodpile....

SISTER FLEETA: *(Sings)*
...Oh Lord you know

I have no friend like you
If heaven's not my home
Oh Lord what will I do
The angels beckon me
From heaven's open door
And I can't feel at home
In this world anymore

(Piano continuing under…)

SISTER FLEETA: Light the sign!

(A neon sign, "THE DOLLHOUSE ORCHESTRA" appears onscreen.)

YUKI: The Dollhouse Orchestra is Sister Fleeta on Hammond B-3 organ, Clarence "Niteowl" Phillips on mouth harp, and Rodney Pinkham Jr. on drums.

SISTER FLEETA: Amateur Nite!

(A neon sign, "AMATEUR NITE," lights up onscreen.)

CRYSTAL: Amateur Nite! All the housewives, nurses, cashiers, businesswomen, college girls and mothers dance onstage, and they got what it takes, each and every one, and their boyfriends, husbands, lovers all shout, smoke Luckies, have a drink with Jim Beam and Mister I W Harper, and the Dollhouse Orchestra plays on…

(CRYSTAL and YUKI join SISTER FLEETA at the piano. Harmony, strong and beautiful.)

CRYSTAL, SISTER FLEETA, & YUKI:
(Sing and play)
Oh Lord you know
I have no friend like you
If heaven's not my home
Oh Lord what will I do
I see angels beckon me
From heaven's open door

and I can't feel at home
In this world anymore...
(Piano continuing)

(CRYSTAL and YUKI dance, sweet and sober. LENNY dances,
RABBI MOSHOWITZ dances. SISTER FLEETA plays on as the
signs fade...)

8.

(Neptune Motel room. STELLA, ZOBELL, dead WINK.)

(YUKI's around...)

YUKI: At the Neptune Motel, beams of golden morning
sunlight stream into the room— and Stella goes
through the pockets of Arthur Wink's corpse for his
Pronto Pizza scooter keys, and the cash in his wallet.

ZOBELL: Stella! Isn't it enough that I killed the poor
bastard? You have to rob him too?

STELLA: The dead don't need money.

ZOBELL: That's not the point.

STELLA: What world do the dead belong to?

ZOBELL: I don't know.

STELLA: The next world. What world does money
belong to? This world, such as it is.
Sixty four bucks. Half is yours.

(STELLA hands ZOBELL the money. They pick up the corpse
between them. Burger King onscreen.)

YUKI: Zobell and Stella drag the body of Arthur Wink
to a dumpster behind Burger King. Nobody around
except a stray dog, who sniffs once at the corpse and
trots away. Same old story.

(Dumpster onscreen. STELLA and ZOBELL swing WINK's
body back and forth.)

STELLA: One and two and three and…

(STELLA *and* ZOBELL *let fly, and* WINK *sails up into the dumpster. He's gone.*)

(MRS PATEL *appears behind her check-in desk.*)

MRS PATEL: Goodbye, Father Christmas.

(ZOBELL *hands* MRS PATEL *some money. And some more.*)

ZOBELL: I'd rather no one knew I'd been here.

MRS PATEL: I am the soul of sexual discretion.

ZOBELL: I just don't want Doctor Berger, or my wife Anna, finding me before I can…

MRS PATEL: Already I don't remember you, sir. I have no room in my brain for you and your teenybopper prostitute.
I was trained as a medical technician in Karachi. Now I am the technician of a fleabag.

STELLA: Its a bitch, lady. Tell it to someone who cares. I'm outta here.

ZOBELL: Where are you going?

STELLA: California. Or Canada. But first I'm taking that Pronto Pizza scooter for a local stop.

ZOBELL: I was hoping you'd help me get to the beach.

STELLA: I can't do that, Mister Zobell. I decided. I'm leaving this crap town now and forever, and I need to see my Mom and Dad first. I got something to say to them, and I hope they have something to say to me.

(STELLA'*s gone. So is* MRS PATEL. *We hear the Pronto Pizza scooter start up and pull away.*)

(ZOBELL *consults a phone book, picks up the phone, dials.*)

ZOBELL: Hello, Mrs Wink?

(MRS WINK, WINK'*s mother, appears. She's in a wheelchair.*)

MRS WINK: That's me.

ZOBELL: Your son Arthur had an accident.

MRS WINK: Who the fuck are you?

ZOBELL: I am no one of interest, Mrs Wink.

MRS WINK: Zat that bitch Stella laughing back there?

ZOBELL: I'm alone, Mrs Wink, sadly enough.

MRS WINK: Where you calling from? The Dollhouse?

ZOBELL: Arthur's dead. A frost grows inside his chest.
I killed him with a metal folding chair, and threw his
body in a dumpster.

MRS WINK: You want something?
You want me to cry into the phone?

ZOBELL: I did think, you know, childhood, a mother's
love.

MRS WINK: The bastard won't come around to steal my
disability checks.
My son Arthur was a worthless drug addict and a
royal pain in the ass. God's joke on me. Whoever you
are, thanks for the news. I can throw away his filthy
clothes, and his record collection. Buddy fucking Holly.

ZOBELL: Goodbye, Mrs Wink. Rave on.

MRS WINK: Hang on a minute. You sound like a decent
guy. You looking for love? Do you believe a woman
of forty-five can still be sexy— even if she's a little
heavyset and has a bad foot. It got bandaged up at the
E R so I'm temporarily on wheels, but I can roll pretty
good, if you get me…

(ZOBELL *hangs up, and* MRS WINK *rolls away.*)

(ZOBELL *moves across the landscape, walking on, video
rolling.*)

(*In another space,* LENNY *with a lantern and a pushbroom.*)

YUKI: Down by the beach, out on the pier, Lenny begins his nitely rounds of the closed attraction— sweep, pick up a little trash, sing a little song.

LENNY: (Sings as he works)
Earth angel, earth angel
Will you be mine?...

YUKI: First star in the west. Sea rolls underneath, kissing the pilings, as it rolled ten thousand years ago...

9.

(ZOBELL walking.)

(UNCLE MONDAY appears in another space, without his sandwich board.)

(CRYSTAL)

CRYSTAL: In these last days, Uncle Monday is seen where and when he wouldn't be seen before. At the moment he's stepping out of the Bag N' Save with a box of donuts, the powdered sugar ones.

(UNCLE MONDAY, holding a donut, notices ZOBELL.)

UNCLE MONDAY: Hey, Pop! Keep picking 'em up and puttin' em down!

ZOBELL: What?

UNCLE MONDAY: Yo' feetz!

CRYSTAL: See! Now Uncle Monday and his doughnuts are up in a tree.

(And so UNCLE MONDAY is, puffing on a short black cigar.)

CRYSTAL: He's smoking a fine De Nobili cigar. His bony long fingered hands look ancient, mummified, like the hands of a dead god. He's feeding donut crumbs to the birds on the branch with him— finches, and they jump like ink drawings of themselves, barely there...

(UNCLE MONDAY *comes down from the tree. He approaches* ZOBELL.)

UNCLE MONDAY: You aint seen a little guy, a fucking dwarf? *(He spits.)* Mister Weenie. He's got a plaid suit. He shops the boys department. Sartorial. The ladies can't get enough.
We used to be associates in the show business. The little bastard is a thief, a liar, a venomous human dwarf being. Soon he will die, by this hand.
You're still on the road, like Jacky Keracky.

ZOBELL: I don't move that fast. The ocean'll be there when I get there.

UNCLE MONDAY: Maybe. Things change.
Hopping and popping.
I'm hoping for employment— Strates, Royal American, hell, any ragbag with a cook tent that'll have me. I'm getting tired of the fixings bar at Fuddruckers.

ZOBELL: What happened to the advertising job?

UNCLE MONDAY: The sandwich board? I was fired. Sister Fleeta felt I was giving the Dollhouse a bad name.

ZOBELL: What are you doing back on this road?

UNCLE MONDAY: Love. It's true love that has me on this stinking strip of blacktop, amid the alien corn.

ZOBELL: Love is a mover. Like the man said, even moves the sun and other stars.

UNCLE MONDAY: I'm not talking cosmodemonic astronomy here. I'm talking Violet Du Bosque, the boss' daughter on Cole Brothers Shows, seventeen, beautiful, a trick shot artist with a bow and arrow. And who did she love, when every man on the show

wanted her? You wouldn't believe it to look at me now,
Mister Zobell, but I was slick. It was Bill and Coo—
until Weenie came along with his Buick Roadmaster,
and pazoo! They drove away together, top down,
headed for God knows where.
She dumped Weenie, married a dentist in Oregon.
Then I heard she was on Park Avenue with an opera
singer. Then she disappeared.
I love her still. I've been searching for her for years,
and that little bastard Weenie's searching too. I heard
he came this way. When our paths cross again, I'll feed
his guts to the seagulls.

(They walk on...)

ZOBELL: Uncle Monday, I hope you find Violet, and she
brings you some happiness in this world...

(SISTER FLEETA appears at her keyboard.)

SISTER FLEETA: *(Sings and plays)*
I am a pilgrim, and a stranger
Traveling thru this wearisome land
I've got a home in yonder city
And its not, not made by hand
(Piano continuing under...)

CRYSTAL: Somebody's playing piano in a house nearby,
rusted tricycle in the front yard, geraniums in a
windowbox...

SISTER FLEETA: *(Sings and plays)*
...I've got a mother, sister and a brother
Who have gone this way before
I am determined to go and see them
For they're on that other shore...
(Piano continuing under)

(UNCLE MONDAY and ZOBELL walk on together.)

CRYSTAL: Our two travelers walk along in silence, each
buried deep in his own thoughts...

UNCLE MONDAY: Onondaga Hotel
Bottle of Canadian Club
Grimy windowpane
Stained glass
Mary washes Christ's feet
With her long black hair
Cold wind, empty streets
City dying under the snow…

ZOBELL: Dead whale on the sand
See the blue shadows the moon makes
In the arch of bones!
Before dawn
Along the beach
Sandpipers skitter on the surfline
First sunlight thru blue fog
There you are, jeans wet to the knee
Smile at me one more time, honey babe,
Light up the world.

SISTER FLEETA: *(Sings and plays)*
I'm going down to the River of Jordan
Just to bathe my wearisome soul
If I can just touch the hem of his garment
Then I know he'd take me home… *(And out)*

(CRYSTAL and SISTER FLEETA are gone. YUKI appears, quietly watching.)

(ZOBELL turns to UNCLE MONDAY.)

ZOBELL: Her name was Lulu. Mademoiselle Electra at Feldman's Amusements. She lived with her Mom in a little house on the river.

(LULU appears in the distance, red bikini, in her electric chair.)

ZOBELL: She always smelled beautiful. Some kinda
perfume. When I asked her the name of it, she
laughed...

LULU: (*Laughs*) You like it? Its called Oriental Flowers.

(LULU *throws the switch, her hair stands on end, blue
sparks. She smiles and waves.*)

ZOBELL: The pier is closed up now. Closed till Kingdom
Come. At which time it re-opens and there she'll be in
that red bikini, sitting in that electric chair...

(LULU *fades, and then she's gone.*)

UNCLE MONDAY: We all lose things in this life, Mister
Zobell. People we love. Our youthful powers.
I used to be a half-ass musician. Now I can't even play
"Come to Jesus" on a hand organ.

ZOBELL: I'm so tired. I gotta rest somewhere.

UNCLE MONDAY: I know just the place.

YUKI: Uncle Monday leads Mister Zobell under a
bridge that crosses a river. Up above the traffic rolls,
but here below it stinks of sewage, dead fish float belly
up on their way downstream...

(UNCLE MONDAY *and* ZOBELL *lie down close to each other.
River sound*)

YUKI: Lying on the muddy bank, they try to sleep. The
sound of the river is everywhere. Hooped round by the
circle of night, they seem the last people in a drowned
world.
Uncle Monday's eyes light up like fireflies in the
gloom...

UNCLE MONDAY: Let me tell you something, kid.
Its fucked. All this local shit. Just pave it over,
intergalactic parking lot. Wake up and watch the first
ships from the Horseshoe Nebula touch down, ever so
lightly...

(Sings)
Under the sycamores, 'bout to rain
Round the curve comes a C & O train
Under that boxcar is Hobo John
He's a lonely hobo, and he's dead and gone...dead and
gone... *(Song ends)*
That's his ghost you're looking at Zobell, in your mind.
Forever riding the rods. Raw deal. Better to get where
you're going, and stay there.

YUKI: Mister Zobell at last falls asleep under the river
bridge. A coal scow drifts by, and then a rowboat with
a Chinese poet, dead drunk at the oars, flower petals
on his white head and on his shoulders. Mister Zobell
is dreaming again...

ZOBELL: A door opens somewhere, and I hear again the
voice of the girl who died long ago. She laughs, and
there's the music of the carousel. The smell of her hair
mixes with the smell of Oriental Flowers perfume, a
heavy scent from the abandoned garden of a Chinese
scholar, overgrown with weeds, broken teacups in the
courtyard...

(In another space, LULU *appears again, this time in the
flowing white dress. Music. She dances, and again the dance
is melancholy, strange, slow...)*

ZOBELL: The archangel Michael brings fire and death
to our enemies, and Gabriel leads the hosts of heaven
in prayer, but who among God's angels will comfort
a poor girl, dead long ago, her bones cold in the deep
waters of the sea...
(Sings)
In the still of the night
I held you, held you tight...

(The music fades. LULU's *gone. River sounds. Darkness)*

10.

(UNCLE MONDAY *and* ZOBELL *walking. In the distance*
RABBI MOSHOWITZ *walks…*)

UNCLE MONDAY: Violet's close. *(He sniffs the air)* Her
scent is on the wind. Once she sees me, she'll rush into
my arms. She'll love me again, won't she? Me and only
me?

ZOBELL: Of course.
She'll see how devoted you are, how you've spent your
life worshipping her, searching for…

UNCLE MONDAY: What if…what if she's become ugly?
Or fat? Or old? What if she's married to a lumberjack?
What if that demon shrimp Weenie is already
whispering his lies into her ear?
She could be in a wheelchair, blind, incontinent…

CRYSTAL: Soon these two philosophers of love arrive
alongside the running track of Lakeview High School.
In the distance, cheerleader practice— seventeen-year
old girls in tiny skirts leap over each other.

CHEERLEADERS: *(From a distance, V O)* Be aggressive! Be
aggressive! B,E, A,G,G,R,E,S,S,I,V,E! Go Panthers, GO!

(RABBI MOSHOWITZ *walks closer, as* CRYSTAL *describes
him.*)

CRYSTAL: Walking slowly around the high school
running track is a man wearing a prayer shawl, a
yarmulke, and a bad suit. The man is muttering to
himself…

RABBI MOSHOWITZ: All is lost! All is lost!

(UNCLE MONDAY *and* ZOBELL *stop and stare at* RABBI
MOSHOWITZ. *He's weeping.*)

ZOBELL: Excuse me. Can we help you?

RABBI MOSHOWITZ: All is lost! Too late…

ZOBELL: Too late for what?

RABBI MOSHOWITZ: His birthday. The Rabbi's birthday.

UNCLE MONDAY: What's the mess, Wes?

RABBI MOSHOWITZ: I am a pilgrim, on my way to the tomb of the great Rabbi Hillel in Jerusalem. The Rabbi only grants blessings at his tomb— and only on his birthday.

UNCLE MONDAY: This is probably a dumb question, but how exactly does he grant blessings if he's dead?

RABBI MOSHOWITZ: Alive, dead. It makes no difference to Rabbi Hillel.

UNCLE MONDAY: My kinda guy.

ZOBELL: When's the Rabbi's birthday?

RABBI MOSHOWITZ: Exactly two months and three days from now. Not enough time to complete my pilgrimage to his holy tomb.

ZOBELL: Uh, I'm not sure the Lakeville High School running track is the road to...

RABBI MOSHOWITZ: Jerusalem, as I'm all too well aware, is across the ocean. I don't have a dime for planefare, or even a rowboat. My pilgrimage is on this quarter mile oval. I count the miles to Jerusalem.
I'm only now approaching Constantinople— lair of the uncircumsized Turk.

UNCLE MONDAY: You, buddy, must be on the same psych meds I am. Stay away from those cut-rate clinics! I'm off. I have my own road, and it ain't to Jerusalem. I'm gonna find that sonofabitch Weenie and rip his little face off. He's probably with her right now, the love of my life, the archery whiz, Miss Violet Du Bosque.
You never seen skin shine like that, under the lights. White satin.

ZOBELL: You'll find her. I know you will.

UNCLE MONDAY: So you say. But what do you know about the way the world wags? You're just a child. Love moves me. I gotta burn the wind. It's been a pleasure talking to you, sweetheart. *(He's gone.)*

YUKI: Uncle Monday runs howling into the great American wilderness...

UNCLE MONDAY: *(O S)* Ooooooooweeeee!

YUKI: ...with Mister Zobell's wallet in his pocket.

ZOBELL: What? *(He fumbles in all his pockets, doesn't find it.)* My wallet! That bastard.

RABBI MOSHOWITZ: Its only money. You need cash, beg on the boulevard. Maybe God will take care of you.

ZOBELL: I'm Abraham Zobell.

RABBI MOSHOWITZ: Rabbi Fred Moshowitz.

ZOBELL: Rabbi, if you're walking to Jerusalem on this running track, how do you know which direction to go?

RABBI MOSHOWITZ: I travel in either direction, counting the miles. There are seven roads to the Holy City of Jerusalem. The Road of Mirrors, the Road of Horn, the Road of Bells...I forget the rest. I'm hoping this is one of them.

Rabbi Hillel will know when I've arrived at his tomb.

(A seagull flies in, lands on RABBI MOSHOWITZ's shoulder. It has a potato chip in its beak. He takes the chip, eats it. The bird shits on his shoulder.)

RABBI MOSHOWITZ: Fucking seagulls.

(RABBI MOSHOWITZ shoos off the gull, brushes off the birdshit.)

(The seagull exits.)

RABBI MOSHOWITZ: Always feeding me, and then flying off with this annoying screech.

SEAGULL *(O S)* Awwwwk!

RABBI MOSHOWITZ: I'm done for the day. Let's go to the synagogue. I can give you some tea.

(As they walk off...)

CHEERLEADERS: *(O S)*
Two, four, six, eight,
Who do we appreciate?
Panthers! Panthers! Yea!!!!

(They walk on. A synagogue in ruins.)

*(*YUKI*)*

YUKI: Rabbi Moshowitz takes Abe Zobell down a dirt road to an abandoned synagogue. The roof is falling in. A pile of dusty prayer books. An altar. Mrs Patel is sweeping up.

MRS PATEL: I know you. Father Christmas.

ZOBELL: Mrs Patel, what are you doing here? Who's running the motel?

MRS PATEL: The Neptune Motel sank into the bog at last. Praise to Ganesha, I escaped with my life. Now I take care of this god-forsaken rabbi and his godforsaken synagogue.
Tell him to pay me.

RABBI MOSHOWITZ: As soon as my disability check arrives.

MRS PATEL: Fucking promised land. I should have stayed in Islamabad. I was a nuclear power engineer. My husband thought we should come to America, get into the motel business. All the laundering, it killed him. Stupid, stupid man.

RABBI MOSHOWITZ: Could you get Mister Zobell a cup
of tea?

MRS PATEL: No more Liptons. The cupboard is bare. A
raccoon is living behind the altar. The droppings are...

RABBI MOSHOWITZ: Enough. *(To* ZOBELL*)*
I once held services here, but now this house of prayer
is a ruin. Mice are gnawing away at the Torah.

ZOBELL: Can I ask— what blessing do you need so
badly that you'll walk five thousand miles to ask a
dead man for it?

RABBI MOSHOWITZ: Forgiveness.
Today I am a poor pilgrim, but I was once the great
Rabbi Fred Moshowitz. I had a loyal congregation
of three thousand souls that listened patiently to
my sermons. They abandoned this schul when they
discovered I was having an affair with a member of my
flock, the wife of a pious man. She was a pleasant idiot,
with big jugs. My wife Miriam walked in on us one day
as I was banging her in the basement of the synagogue.
By the furnace, God forgive me.
Miriam threatened me. She said she would tell the
congregation, the newspapers— unless I gave her a
lot of money. I knew that if I gave it to her once, she
would come back for more.
I arranged for Miriam to be murdered in our house,
in what looked like a robbery. I paid an evil man
ten thousand dollars to do this. He killed her, and
was caught the next day robbing a Sunoco station.
He confessed, and I went to prison for twenty years.
During that time I studied the Zohar and the Book of
Lights and Towers for ten hours every day. I found
nothing to help me.

My life is a pointless history of selfishness, stupidity,
and misery.
May I ask you a question?

ZOBELL: Anything.

RABBI MOSHOWITZ: I see a sick old man, walking slowly along the side of the road. He's not a hobo, or a drunk. Mister Zobell, toward what holy shrine does my fellow pilgrim point his steps?

ZOBELL: The beach. A girl I loved died in that ocean long ago. I'm going to say some final words to her, scatter some flowers on the sea.

(RABBI MOSHOWITZ looks ZOBELL over. Then suddenly he begins laughing, more and more hysterically.)

(Finally he pulls himself together.)

ZOBELL: What's the joke?

RABBI MOSHOWITZ: You.
You'll drown yourself in that ocean.
And you don't even know it.

ZOBELL: That's crazy.

RABBI MOSHOWITZ: Is it now?

ZOBELL: That's not what I…

RABBI MOSHOWITZ: The dead, Mister Zobell— they want company. Its lonely in the grave. They want to talk over old times. And they never shut up, not ever, until they wrap their cold arms around their lovers, and never let go.

ZOBELL: Please. Please don't….

RABBI MOSHOWITZ: Abraham Zobell! Stop listening to the voices in your head for one fucking moment. Listen to me.
Guilt is as worthless as grief, as worthless as regret. I know, as I've been the slave of these three goddesses all my life.
Their sweet song— lies, Mister Zobell. Nonsense
(Sings)
Halloo, halloo, loo loo!

Go home, let yourself heal. Live whatever life remains to you.

ZOBELL: It's too late for that now.

(RABBI MOSHOWITZ *shrugs*.)

RABBI MOSHOWITZ: Pilgrims are persistent bastards. Do you know where we are, Mister Zobell? Babylon. By the rivers of Babylon, to be more precise. And we weep, when we remember Jerusalem.
What will happen to us when we arrive? At Jerusalem or at the seaside. Will we be forgiven? Will we be changed?
Think it over. Meanwhile, I'm off to Sister Fleeta's Dollhouse.

MRS PATEL: Nasty, nasty place. Boogie-woogie. I don't approve.

RABBI MOSHOWITZ: Mrs Patel, the life force will not be denied.

MRS PATEL: Poor excuse for leering at young women in small costumes.

RABBI MOSHOWITZ: And drinking.

MRS PATEL: Go then. What do I care? Make a fool of yourself on the dancing floor.

RABBI MOSHOWITZ: I always do.
Tonight is Amateur Night. The Dollhouse Orchestra! Come along, Mister Zobell. Every pilgrim needs a break.

(*They're gone.* MRS PATEL *is gone in the opposite direction.* YUKI *alone*.)

(*In another space,* LENNY *appears…*)

YUKI: Meanwhile, out on the pier, Lenny once again makes his final round of all the shuttered attractions. Then he retires to his small room at the far end, where only thin floorboards separate him from the ocean below.

(LENNY *turns on a tinny radio, a doo-wop era instrumental— Tequila, or Telstar, or Bumble Boogie. We can hear the waves below. He cracks a beer, lights up a smoke.*)

YUKI: He has a pile of old National Geographics in there, a few issues of Playboy, cans of franks and beans, a hotplate, a sixpack of Kingfisher and a carton of Camel straights. Home sweet home. Later tonight, the Dollhouse!

11.

(Sister Fleeta's Dollhouse)

(Near the dancefloor— ZOBELL with RABBI MOSHOWITZ. UNCLE MONDAY. Present in a more ghostly way, upstage— LENNY, LULU, NAT FELDMAN.)

(Drinking, smoking, laughing)

(The Dollhouse Orchestra plays— mouthharp, drums, Sister Fleeta on keyboards.)

SISTER FLEETA & BAND
(Sing and play)
Hand me down my walking cane
Hand me down my walking cane
Hand me down my walking cane
Lord, I'm leaving on the midnight train
All my sins are taken away

(Go-go dancing onstage— CRYSTAL and YUKI in their dancing outfits, glittery and sexy.)

SISTER FLEETA & BAND:
Well, hand me down my rocking shoes
Hand me down my rocking shoes
Lord, hand me down my rocking shoes

We're gonna rock away the blues
All my sins are taken away
(Music continuing under...)

(CRYSTAL comes over to RABBI MOSHOWITZ, and drags him up onstage to dance.)

(SISTER FLEETA is pounding the piano. The band is wailing. RABBI MOSHOWITZ dances with CRYSTAL...)

(The music grows louder, more insistent...)

SISTER FLEETA & BAND:
Well, hand me down my walking bone
Hand me down my walking bone
Lord, hand me down my walking bone
It's so hard to be alone
All my sins are taken away...
(Music continuing under...)

(YUKI drags ZOBELL up to dance. He stands shakily, then begins to dance, harder and faster, inspired by Yuki and the music.)

(ZOBELL dances wildly, then clutches his chest.)

(The music stops suddenly.)

(Lights go slowly to black as, in slow motion, ZOBELL collapses to the floor.)

(Lights back up. Everyone is gone but CRYSTAL, SISTER FLEETA, YUKI, and ZOBELL.)

(ZOBELL is in SISTER FLEETA's arms.)

(Pieta)

(He's still breathing.)

(SISTER FLEETA smokes a cigarette.)

(CRYSTAL and YUKI watch over them.)

(Dead quiet...)

SISTER FLEETA: Time will take you on, sweetheart, be you a king on his golden throne, or a beggar by the side of the road. Nothing in this world as strong as the gentle hands of Time...

ZOBELL: I'm dying...

SISTER FLEETA: Don't be so damn quick to dance with Yuki. It ain't easy to keep up with her.

ZOBELL: Dying...
And I'm only a little boy...

SISTER FLEETA: Quiet now, Mister Abe Zobell. You're not dying. Not yet.
In fact, you gotta be on your way. The Dollhouse is closing up.

(CRYSTAL *and* YUKI *help* ZOBELL *to stand. He's shaky, but he can do it.*)

(*Sister Fleeta's Dollhouse fades away around him.*)

(CRYSTAL *and* SISTER FLEETA *are gone.*)

(YUKI *watches as* ZOBELL *takes a hesitant step forward... and another...*)

12.

(YUKI *and* ZOBELL. *He walks, slow but steady.*)

YUKI: On the road, deep middle of the night, Zobell alone...

(ZOBELL *turns to the audience.*)

ZOBELL: My name is Abraham Zobell.
I am standing under a streetlight On the Neptune Parkway.
In the east, no trace of dawn
It's raining.
Droplets fly in the streetlight.
My name is Zobell.
My name is written in salt, Dissolves away in the rain.

(We see LENNY *in another space, out on the pier, holding a lantern. Carousel music. The shadows of the horses…)*

ZOBELL: Give yourself to the sea

A gentle fall

So easy

A mouthful of blood and a sigh

Held in the arms of the waves

*(*LENNY*'s gone. The music and horse shadows fade.)*

*(*ARTHUR WINK'S GHOST *appears in the road.)*

ARTHUR WINK'S GHOST: Zobell! Its you, still looking like shit warmed over.

ZOBELL: Arthur Wink. Stella's ex-boyfriend. Aren't you…dead?

ARTHUR WINK'S GHOST: Damn straight I am. You killed me, threw me in a fucking dumpster.

ZOBELL: I had no choice. You were about to…

ARTHUR WINK'S GHOST: Hey. I'm not gonna apologize for behaving like an asshole. A snake will bite, every time. What the fuck was I supposed to do? Be someone else?

ZOBELL: You could have been yourself, but with a little improvement.

ARTHUR WINK'S GHOST: Yeah, well. Doesn't matter now. I got a situation here. I'm trying to get out of this world, but I seem to have been left behind - sort of in between. A screw-up.

ZOBELL: What's it like in the afterlife? Do you see God? Do you?

ARTHUR WINK'S GHOST: Are you deaf? Don't you get it? I can't tell you shit about the afterlife, as I can't seem to get there.

I'm somewhere else. Not here. I can't say where
exactly.

I need money for bus-fare.

(ZOBELL *gives* ARTHUR WINK'S GHOST *some cash.*)

ZOBELL: Are you sure you're dead?

ARTHUR WINK'S GHOST: I'll get there. Eventually.
Peace. Torment. Whatever.
It's a bitch, Mister Zobell, any way you look at it.

ZOBELL: Maybe so.

ARTHUR WINK'S GHOST: I gotta get down to the
Trailways Depot.

(ARTHUR WINK'S GHOST *heads off. Before he's gone, he
turns back to* ZOBELL.)

ARTHUR WINK'S GHOST: Rave on. (*He's gone.*)

(ZOBELL *walks, slow, exhausted, in pain. Video rolls.*)

(*At the side of the road by a tree,* UNCLE MONDAY. *He's
lying in a twisted position, blood on his head and face.*)

(CRYSTAL)

CRYSTAL: Uncle Monday! This time he's lying by the
side of the road. He's had an accident…a bad one.

(ZOBELL *kneels down by* UNCLE MONDAY, *looks at his head
wound.*)

ZOBELL: What happened? Are you…

UNCLE MONDAY: Goddamn tractor-trailer clipped me.
Musta been doing eighty, the wind knocks me off my
feet and I slam into the ass end as the fucker booms by.

ZOBELL: The cut's deep, I can see the bone. You need an
ambulance. There's a…

UNCLE MONDAY: Nah. My head's cracked open, that's
all. I'm all right. Its not bleeding so much anymore.
Just prop me up against this tree.

(With some effort, ZOBELL does so. UNCLE MONDAY grins at him.)

UNCLE MONDAY: This kind of thing, it happens all the time.

You know something? That little son of a bitch Weenie, he can make a quart of wine disappear while everyone else is still looking for the corkscrew…

ZOBELL: Uncle Monday, I should call an ambulance. Your head is…

UNCLE MONDAY: Those sirens are loud enough to wake the dead. Besides, I don't want to make trouble for nobody. You need to get to the beach, don't you? You go on. I'm fine.

(UNCLE MONDAY waves ZOBELL away, pointing down the road. ZOBELL doesn't move.)

(UNCLE MONDAY coughs and moans. Then he's quiet for a long breath.)

UNCLE MONDAY: Are you…you still here?

ZOBELL: I'm here.

UNCLE MONDAY: I can't see anymore. It's dark. *(He moans again, and then quiet…)* You still here?

ZOBELL: I'm here.

UNCLE MONDAY: Then take my hand, Mister Zobell. I'm dying.

(ZOBELL takes UNCLE MONDAY's hand, then kneels down and cradles him in his arms.)

UNCLE MONDAY: It's hard…to know…I'll never see her face again… *(He is still.)*

13.

(Night. ZOBELL *moving slow, unsteady.* CRYSTAL *and* YUKI *watch him.)*

ZOBELL: Black dog howls under the pier
The wind is nothing but a whisper now
Her back warm beneath the dress
Her tongue in my mouth—
I'm hanging
On a thin rope of blood
Then the railroad crossing bell,
Sweet and insistent,
Red lights
The barrier lowers
Distant heartbeat of the train
Just visible
Blowing smoke at the tip of the curve
Arcata, blue fog on the beach…
Anna's face glows in the mirror…
(Sings, with difficulty)
As I wander…through this world,
Nothing…can stop the Duke of Earl…

*(*ZOBELL *stops singing, stops moving. He's so weak he can't take another step. He's about to fall to the ground.)*

(Car horn sounds. Headlights on ZOBELL.*)*

CRYSTAL: Wouldn't you know it. Stella shows up. Right on time.

YUKI: In a big fucking Buick.

*(*STELLA *appears, and a Buick fills the screen.)*

STELLA: Need a lift?

ZOBELL: *(With difficulty)* Stella…I was about to lie down on this blacktop…wait for an ambulance to pick me up…

STELLA: Or run you over.
Get in.

(STELLA *helps* ZOBELL *into the car. He collapses into the seat.*)

(*Off they go.*)

(*Video rolls at a driving clip…*)

ZOBELL: How'd you find me?

STELLA: Cruising all up and down this road. I figured if you hadn't made it to the ocean yet, I could still help you out.

ZOBELL: Where'd you get this big ass car?

STELLA: I stole it.

ZOBELL: Stella, you can't just…

STELLA: It's my Dad's. He doesn't know I took it.

(STELLA *keeps driving. A silence between them as* ZOBELL *recovers.*)

ZOBELL: Stella….I don't want you to drive me all the way.
I've walked so far. After I rest a little, I want to take the last steps on my own.

STELLA: Have it your way, Mister Zobell.

ZOBELL: I want to get there when the sun is just rising out of the sea.

YUKI: It's still dark. They need to kill some time. Stella parks under an overpass.
Zobell sleeps, exhausted.
Stella stays awake, smokes, watches the night…

STELLA: (*Sings*)
The cool autumn breeze
Sends a chill down my spine…

(CRYSTAL *and* YUKI *look out toward the ocean.*)

CRYSTAL: Down by the beach, lights flicker on the closed amusement pier.

(Again, music and the shadows of carousel horses. This time the shadows are huge, frightening.)

YUKI: The carousel. Its moving. Someone's turned it on.

(Huge shadow horses, slowly at first, begin to turn and turn…circling the stage and the entire inside of the theater.)

(Distant carousel music)

CRYSTAL: It's Lenny. He's riding, all by himself…

(Distant sound of LENNY's laughter…)

YUKI: …riding on through the night, his beard flying back in the breeze. He's laughing…and laughing….

(LENNY's laughter and the carousel music fades, along with the circling shadows of the horses.)

14.

(STELLA and ZOBELL in the Buick.)

(CRYSTAL and YUKI)

CRYSTAL: Stella pulls over.

(The Buick slows, stops.)

STELLA: The beach is about a half mile. This road hits it right at the old amusement pier.

ZOBELL: Almost there. And still alive. Thanks to you.

STELLA: I wouldn't have made it if I hadn't met you. No chance.
I love you, Mister Zobell, always and forever, till I die.

(STELLA puts her arms around ZOBELL, hugs him hard. She kisses his cheek with great tenderness. Then she lets him go.)

STELLA: I'm going to California in this car and never coming back. You can come if you want to.

ZOBELL: No, thanks.

STELLA: Take very good care of yourself, Mister Zobell.

(STELLA's gone. Buick's gone.)

(ZOBELL alone. Video rolls slow.)

CRYSTAL: Zobell walks along the Neptune parkway
through the morning. Kids in a red convertible blow
past him, doing seventy. Little old man at a bus stop
waves— and lights the stump of a cigar…

At last, he reaches the boardwalk, frozen custard
stands shut for the winter, shutters flap in the wind.
Bright sunlight on the sea.

(A long silence as ZOBELL looks out at the pier and the
ocean. Then, fading in slowly, sound of surf. Gulls)

ZOBELL: Paladin, Paladin, where do you roam?

Whatever is given me.

Thy will be done.

CRYSTAL: Smoke. The smell of smoke. The pier is
on fire. Feldman's Amusements— the carousel, the
octopus, all of it. There it goes!
The Haunted Castle catches fire. Flames lick up the
sky.

YUKI: Its Lenny!

CRYSTAL: He's caught in the fire!

(LENNY appears, spinning and whirling, all his clothes on
fire. He bangs at the flames with his hands. He sees ZOBELL
on the beach.)

LENNY: Hiya, kid! I'm burning up!

YUKI: His beard's on fire!

CRYSTAL: Lenny burns, turns into a flake of ash, drifts
high up into the sky over the pier, and out over the
ocean. He's gone.

(LENNY *disappears.*)

YUKI: The Haunted Castle, dry as tinder, is a tower of flame. The pier itself starts to blacken from the heat. White flakes of ash in the wind, like giant snowflakes... Fire over water.

ZOBELL: What's that out on the waves? A boat, its ragged sail in shreds.
At the helm is Baba Yaga, Death's witch. Her eyes are whirling blue pinwheels. She's screaming my name into the wind. The boat of the dead.
On board are Arthur Wink, Uncle Monday— and there's Lulu, risen up from where she rides on the endless currents undersea...all beckoning, calling me...

(ZOBELL *stands motionless, looking out at the burning pier, the boat of the dead, and the ocean.*)

ZOBELL: Cry these dreadful summoners grace.

(*Sound of the surf. A long moment*)

ZOBELL: A girl who once loved me is gone,
Back into the sea.
Only the endless roar of the surf remains
First sunlight thru blue fog,
There you are, Anna, jeans wet to the knee
Smile at me one more time, honey babe,
Light up the world.

15.

(ANNA *is there.*)

ANNA: ABE! Abe!

(ZOBELL *turns to* ANNA.)

YUKI: And the boat of the dead has disappeared into the glare of the rising sun.

A black crow flies low over the sea, dips its wings in the salt water. The pier burns.

ANNA: Abe, it's me. I found you.

ZOBELL: I did it, Anna. I saw the ocean. One last time.

ANNA: Yes, Abe. You did it.

ZOBELL: Anna, I....

ANNA: Tell me later, Abe. I want to hear it all.
Now we're going home.

(ANNA *and* ZOBELL *walk off together slowly, he leaning on her. As they do so,* SISTER FLEETA *appears.* CRYSTAL *and* YUKI)

SISTER FLEETA: (*Sings and plays*)
Oh let me fly, oh let me fly
Let me fly to Mount Zion, Lord, Lord...
(*Continuing under*)

(ANNA *and* ZOBELL *are gone.*)

SISTER FLEETA:
Way down yonder in the middle of the field,
Angel working at the chariot wheel,
Not so particular 'bout working at the wheel,
Just want to see how the chariot feel
Oh let me fly, oh let me fly
Let me fly to Mount Zion, Lord, Lord...
(*Continuing under softly*)

(ANNA and ZOBELL's living room at home. He is back in his armchair, she is asleep on the couch.

YUKI: That evening
The first snow of winter falls
From on high
Translucent flakes
Invisible in the dark

Under the streetlights they gather
Drift down tinted gold.
You can see them there
Close to the earth.
They touch,
Melt and disappear
Back to the formless, to the One
Behind this universe of forms.
The snow stops, clouds dissolve,
The vault of heaven is infinite,
Radiant with stars.
Below the lights of Hidden River, and the glow of New
Jerusalem Beyond the hills.
From time to time
a star breaks loose from its sphere and arcs across the
sky.

CRYSTAL: The House of Zobell is warm, gentle sound
of Anna's breathing, her beautiful face on the pillow,
white hair falling round it like a flower...
A cup of tea grows cold next to him... the ocean in his
head, waves rolling forever, on and on and on...

ZOBELL: Someone's in the mirror. A fool in the forest,
lost, the bells on his cap tinkle. Night falls.
That's the end of Zobell's Amusements, burned away
in fire- nothing more to say, not this time around, not
in this life, not under this sun—
(Sings)
Duke duke duke, duke of earl
Duke duke, duke of earl...

END PLAY

(SISTER FLEETA comes downstage center slowly, dark
glasses, her cane tapping the floor before her.)

SISTER FLEETA:
What does it matter
What you say?
Just the peeping of baby birds in the nest
Calling for their mother.

This dark and bright world rolls on through space.
There was trouble at its making-a twist in the creation,
something cracked, missing. This world was made
while God was dreaming— and it will never again
come right, not ever, not until the end of time.

Pray for us. Keep on.

www.ingramcontent.com/pod-product-compliance
Lightning Source LLC
Chambersburg PA
CBHW052216090426
42741CB00010B/2566